Amazon Echo User Guide

By Jack Echo

CONTENTS

CHAPTER 1 – HAVE YOU MET ALEXA?

Amazon Echo is yet another breakthrough in today's world of ever-changing and ever-evolving technology brought to you by Amazon. When it comes to living in a smart and efficient world, this revolutionary gadget hits the nail on the head. Amazon has been gradually and quietly developing Echo deep within its well renowned Lab126 offices located in Silicon Valley and Cambridge, Massachusetts. For a period of four consecutive years, they have been tinkering and modifying the wonderful Amazon Echo in their labs. This impressive device which initially had the code name 'Project D' or 'Doppler', was part of Amazon's very first endeavor to expand their portfolio of smart gadgets beyond the original Kindle E-reader (which was a revolutionary pioneer in its own right).

In order for you to have a much better comprehension of the intentions of Amazon here, you have to take into consideration their overall business model. Amazon is in the trade of providing you with virtually everything that you require, starting from basic necessities such as clothes and groceries to luxurious yet fundamental items including electronics and more. Amazon also offers a wide range of gifts and anything else in-between; therefore, Amazon tends to be a one stop shop for most, if not all of our requirements. In order for Amazon to accomplish this more efficiently and provide an even higher level of service for us, they need to know more about you, your family and your friends. By having this information about you, your family, and your friends, they will have the ability to make better and more precise recommendations of items for you to buy taking into account your shopping habits and preferences. The more accurate these recommendations (also taking into account their within your price range!), this increases the chances of you accepting their recommendations which saves you valuable time and your decision making power (unless of course you love window shopping).

This highly innovative product serves as a hybrid speaker with an excellent voice recognition feature that has the ability to answer a variety of questions and perform particular tasks, thanks to the personal voice assistant, Alexa. Alexa is Amazon's response to Google Now, Microsoft's Cortana and Apple's Siri, which all come as standard features with a variety of smartphones today. Alexa is the sign of huge things to come as successful technology firms and organizations are convinced our future will comprise of talking to intelligent computers that make our lives easier and stress-free.

The Age of Intelligent Personal Assistants is here and Alexa Stands Out From the Crowd!

It has been decades since our generation has become completely hooked and fascinated by visions of the future. Movies, plays, music and fiction novels as well as other forms of literary works have mirrored our enthrallment to the idea of having highly advanced technology that offers capabilities our current minds find very hard to comprehend.

Never far from these mental images of a technology driven future are sights of computers and the near superhuman characteristics we imagine them to possess in the future. Take for example entertaining the idea of flying cars that drive you through floating residential and commercial spaces with you constantly communicating to a virtual companion who knows exactly where you are, the things you want to do, plans out your daily activities, plays your favorite tunes, knows personal details about you, your family, relatives and close friends, and with a simple prompt activated by your voice can provide you answers to any query you have. Well we haven't arrived at that point in the future yet but we have been given sweet samplers for a taste of this fun, gratifying, and leisurely set up coming our way in the near future.

Out to offer us taste tests of this future we have close at hand Apple's Siri, Microsoft's Cortana, Samsung's S Voice, Windows Brainasoft's Braina, Cognitive Code's SILVIA, and Google's Google Now, just to name a few of the latest innovations on Intelligent Personal Assistants (IPAs). Among this group of forerunners in the era of intelligent responding computers, let us not forget the sassy girl we have just been introduced to, Amazon's brilliant Alexa.

Intelligent Personal Assistants are a group of software agents that demonstrate a level of artificial intelligence by carrying out particular tasks for its user. These specific pieces of work are grounded on the IPA's interaction with the user, by the information the individual feeds the device, its ability to use Global Positioning System (GPS) to determine its present location, and its inherent capacity to gain access to a myriad of information from several sources on the internet.

What set these IPAs apart from other common group computing devices is its unique and similar characteristics it shares with human beings. These devices function in a manner that would make us easily believe that they are indeed capable of higher level intelligence such as reasoning, learning, planning, and comprehending.

Quite obviously, Intelligent Personal Assistants can be put to use in an indefinite number of settings such as during ordinary daily routines (for organizing a shopping list, updating a calendar and/or maintaining a checklist of things to do), in work scenarios it can be used to perform emails, calls or schedule trackers. These IPAs can even be utilized to help out with looking up items on the internet for reference or quick trivial inquiries.

This breakthrough technology is still in its infancy whilst developers are continuously discovering innovative capacities, skills, and functions to integrate into the device for it to become more alive with personality. Like a toddler learning to talk, walk and potty, the IPAs are still figuring out more of its capabilities. And as software engineers and programmers continue to find ways of improving the IPAs, persistently pushing the limits of what is technologically viable for these devices, we will definitely see more of these innovations and these IPAs are definitely here to keep us company for many years to come. After all, envisioning a future where humans constantly communicate with computers isn't such a hard thought to stomach these days is it?

As sure as the earth's rotation on its axis, our sweet girl Alexa is without question here to stick with us for the long run. In a matter of weeks since her exclusive debut to premiere members of the Amazon community in November 2014, Alexa has been the talk of the town and has been making quite the noise among enthusiasts and common folk alike. Now that Amazon has made her more accessible for more households, the interest for her has ridiculously escalated. The computer and technology community have been raving about all the things she is capable of (which we will talk about in more detail in the following chapters of this book), and all the promising talents she has got hidden inside her sleek solid frame.

What makes Alexa stand out from the rest of the exclusive IPA circle is its attractive and simple aesthetics. Its female voice simulation sounds more natural when compared alongside its counterparts. Alexa's response time is relatively quick with a great deal of functionality that we will talk more in detail about later. The microphones are extremely sensitive, allowing easier recognition and comprehension of your voice even when background noises are in the way. Has the capability of connecting with household lighting facility and therefore gives you the ability to turn your home's lighting on or off without having to lift a finger. It can turn itself into a cool Bluetooth speaker that will play any audio you want to hear or turn it into a prime quality radio playing your favorite tunes from your very own playlists. And with all these functionalities, you can get Alexa to do this for you and all you have to do is ask, literally.

Is Amazon Echo All Talk?

This is the question you might be struggling with the first time you take a glance at it. The incorporated features we'll cover in finer detail later in this guide will make you realize that this is the ultimate gadget for a smart person in a smart world. In today's world, everything needs to be smarter than average. There is a need for devices to be connected to something or better yet, be connected to everything that we interact with. What is even more inspiring is that it gets easier when we can talk directly to these items without having to fumble with knobs or buttons.

With Alexa, the question isn't what can she do? It should be "What can't Alexa do?" On one hand you have an exceptional portable speaker that ties into all the largest music streaming services (Pandora and iTunes) which of course includes Amazon Music Library and Prime Music as well. Recently, two of the world's most listened to music streaming radios have also tied up with the Amazon Echo, expanding the list of stations you can choose good music from. iHeartRadio and TuneIn have just jumped in the band wagon of the ever growing music library options of Amazon Echo. With all these huge online radio stations backing up Echo's ability to give out good quality music, you will never have to struggle to look for that particular song you heard ten years ago during your sister's brother-in-law's wedding.

On the other hand, you have an interactive helper who will perform tasks for you such as making shopping, setting up alarms and timers and to-do lists ultra-simplified. You get to create a schedule and input it into Google's calendar. Whenever you feel dazed off and all over the place because of all the stresses of the day, no need to fuss, simply ask Alexa your remaining schedule for the day and go through your activities with fewer worries. Shopping has also never been made simpler, because Echo is conveniently connected to Amazon's comprehensive online market, again all you have to do is ask Alexa to do the shopping for you and expect the items to be delivered to your front door in no time.

A new addition to the features of the Echo involves the use of *Audible* that allows you to listen to audiobooks. Now you can continue your progress with a book you have been reading anywhere in your home, as long as you can still clearly hear Alexa's voice.

The Amazon Echo is undeniably an indispensable addition to the household, making simple household routines come alive with life because of its unique functionalities. Since Echo's compatibility with Belkin WeMo, Philips Hue and Wink household devices, you get to control your home without having to move so much as a muscle. Simply picture this, it's a snowy December evening and a family member has asked you to turn the garage lights outside for them but you've been slouched comfortably in your living room curled up with a good book, hot chocolate, and are feeling much too lazy to get up. No problem. Just ask Alexa to turn the lights on for you, and why not pitch in an additional request of dimming your lamp shade and turning up the room heater for a more relaxing reading experience?

Other useful features of the Echo include traffic and weather inquiries. Along with updates on the latest news and current events, real time sports scores and upcoming game schedules. There really is no limit with the things you can ask Alexa, especially now that it can get its information from Wikipedia, and it is smart enough to even answer simple mathematical operations or even unit conversions.

This is really just the tip of the iceberg with the boss' new personal assistant called Alexa though.

The Amazon Echo could seemingly give the impression of being a bit of an odd product to some people however with it becoming widely available in late June 2015, it is sure to be a staple in most people's households. When Alexa finally arrives at your door beautifully dressed and ready to rock and roll (or if you already have her!), after a few minutes of setting her up, you will get to explore the serious potential that this device holds which will continuously improve long into the future.

CHAPTER 2 - WHAT'S THIS AMAZON ECHO I KEEP HEARING ABOUT?

Amazon Echo is a cleverly contrived speaker infused with cutting edge interactive technology in order to make today's life much simpler. This well-designed speaker comes with a merit of its user friendly voice control system, which is anchored by the smooth-sounding and soothing "Alexa," this swift gadget is designed around the sound of your voice. It's always on (plugged into an electric socket) and you are only required to ask it for information such as; news, weather, music, and much more and it will happily respond with an answer. Echo will start working the moment it hears you mention the wake word, "Alexa.", if this wake word causes issues in your house (such as a family or friend who's called Alexa, then you can change the wake word to "Amazon" – more on this later). The Echo is essentially a hybrid of a cross between Siri and Sonos having a baby, and results in a smart speaker that can recite a mountain of information or play wonderful music that will calm or blow your mind into a dancing fury.

In simpler terms, the Amazon Echo is a cool speaker that contains an in-built voice assistant which works like a more advanced version of Apple's Siri or Microsoft's Cortana. Rather than being an anything for anytime virtual helper, like what the smart phones are offering, Echo has been specifically built to be useful within a home environment. It's able to do everything from working as an alarm clock to wake you up in the morning (or from naps) to assisting you in building up a check list for groceries, and conveying weather forecasts, or the latest news.

There is quite a lot to admire about the Echo apart from Amazon's merger of a natural language savvy personal assistant and a connected Bluetooth speaker making it the latest futuristic appliance to enter the consumer market. This device is a smart speaker with cloud connectivity that you can control by your own voice or via a mobile application for Kindle Fire, Android or iOS. This piece of marvelous technology also has a mic-enabled remote control that is similar to the one that comes with the Fire TV.

Beyond all that, the Amazon Echo 'brain' is connected to the cloud (or the internet) so that it is easily and automatically upgraded and improved (without you having to do a thing!) through the cloud when Amazon releases new updates and upgrades. This sole functionality that Amazon has built in to the device means there is no upper limit as to what the Amazon Echo can do long in to the future, considering Amazon continues improving upon it (which Amazon has no doubt a highly vested interest in doing – especially once similar products come on the market to compete with the Echo).

How does the Amazon Echo work?

How is it possible for the device to understand what I say?

And how does it form the right answers to my questions?

The Amazon Echo has been dubbed as the "Computer of the Future" because of its ability to respond to human formulated questions and commands with so much ingenuity using a fluid, natural sounding voice and under a very fast response time. These qualities have made the experience feel like you are talking to an almost human device. The question resides and remains perplexing in our heads: How does Alexa do all these?

The close-to-human voice of Alexa with very impressive mastery of the English language can be ascribed to the power of Natural Language Process (NLP) coupled with the Text-to-Speech (TTS) technology. The Echo's ability to comprehend human inquiries and commands can be attributed to the NLP and the TTS is in charge of converting computational knowledge into human audible language.

NLP is concerned with the study of the interaction of humans with computers. With this comprehensive study, experts were able to develop sets of algorithms to translate human thoughts, mannerisms and speech into numbers and figures – the form of language that computers can easily digest and understand. Once set up, the geeks who invented the Echo then incorporated in Echo a set of programs that prompts it to respond in a certain manner once it was fed with information through human speech. In order for the device to give out an answer that is useful for ordinary humans, the device must then use the TTS capability imbedded in it to convert computer language to human language. Once the human being received his or her answer, communication has now lapsed between man and computer.

Relevant Privacy Issues

A number of critiques have been focused on finding fault in pointing out how closely the Amazon Echo listens into the conversations of household members. Questions have been raised regarding the Echo's quality of always being on and always listening to people inside the house. The biggest issue is the fear that the Echo might be stepping into personal boundaries, or have already stepped over the boundaries, of human privacy.

Echo has been given unlimited access into secret conversations inside the comforts of the owner's own home, even other non-verbal objects (such as doors) can't escape the consistent monitoring of the Echo and this feature sort of freaks out some critics and reviewers. Echo is able to "intelligently" determine the number of people in the house, where they are headed or staying, their predictable actions and where they would be headed or be at a particular point in time and this may greatly compromise a person's safety.

Being the devil's advocate, if in the hands of the wrong people the information conveniently stored and locked inside the Echo could well may be used negatively and could speak a hundred levels of harm to another person. All it takes is the malicious intent and access to the Echo app of the person or family, which by the way is also very conveniently tied up to the "Cloud".

Amazon's response to these fears is the assurance that Echo will only stream the recorded conversations when the wake word is triggered and that Amazon Echo is geared up into action. On the same note, Amazon has legally bounded both their company and the user to a Privacy Notice and both parties can be deemed liable for dire consequences in the event of a breach of contract.

CHAPTER 3 - WHAT'S IN THE BOX?

The Amazon Echo comes in a well-furnished box that has a bright orange interior, similar to all Fire products sold by Amazon. In the box, you will find the Echo (a.k.a. Alexa), a voice-capable remote control unit with batteries included and an AC power cord. All these accessories come wrapped individually for protective purposes. Along with the accessories, there is a set-up guide that comes with a glossary of commands and questions that Alexa can comprehend (which is ever increasing).

The Amazon Echo itself is a fine satin black cylindrical device with a height of, 9.25 inches and a diameter of 3.25 inches. Most of the weight of the Echo is brought about by the in-built speaker and amplifier, which outputs sound. The Echo is rather heavy for its size considering there are no rechargeable batteries built into it and this is a clear cut sign of a solidly built device.

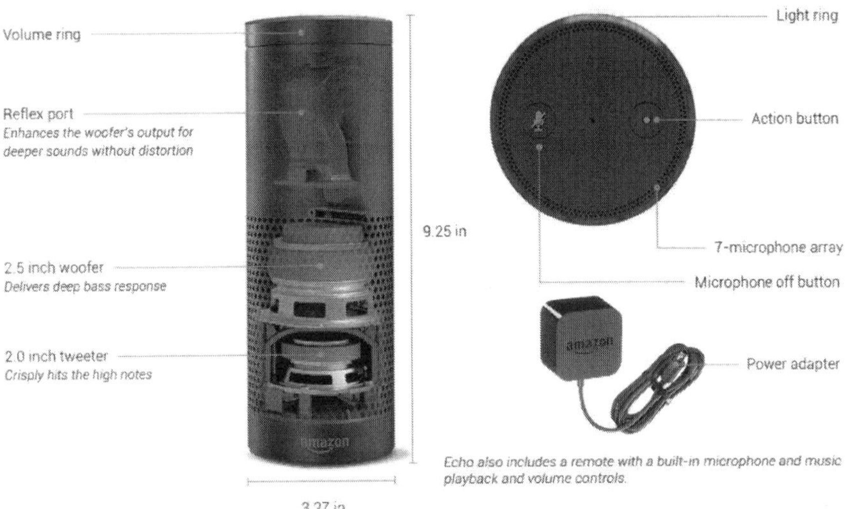

The Aesthetics

The Echo tends to work only on AC power which you may think of as a limitation but is quite sensible in the grand scheme of things since it needs a lot of power for continuous listening and amplification of sound. On the top of the Echo there's a button for setting up a new location as well as a button for muting sounds. The top half-inch of the Amazon Echo is easily rotated to adjust the volume of the speaker.

Even though the Amazon Echo connects to a home

network via Wi-Fi, it has to be plugged into an electrical outlet in a stationary position since it does not come with batteries. Unlike other wireless speakers on the market, the black Echo has a very simple design. The only time the device emits light is during interaction periods; a multi-colored ring of light emerges at the top of the device during each interaction which soon fades away shortly after.

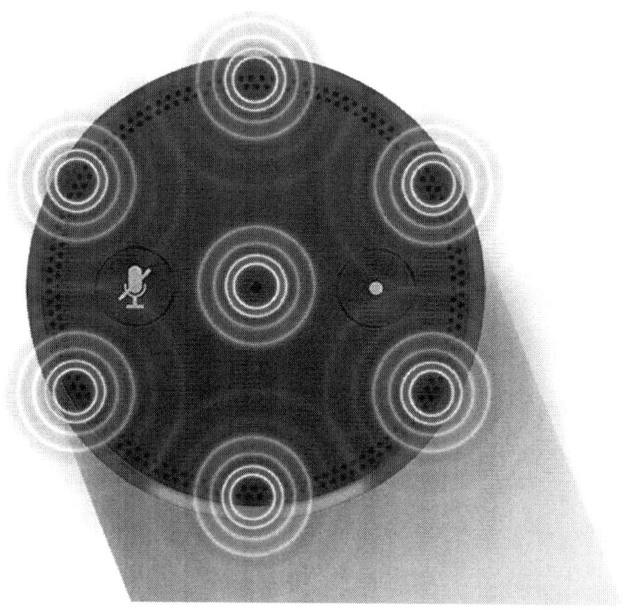

Near the bottom of the Echo, there is a power LED that turns solid white once the device has connected to the Wi-Fi network and when it isn't connected, the LED emits a solid orange. The Echo contains seven microphone sensors which are located at various points around the ring of light (see above). These microphone sensors make use of "beam-forming technology" enabling it to listen for sounds from any given direction. In addition, it possesses noise canceling capabilities, allowing Alexa to be an outstanding listener (perhaps more so than your husband or wife) as background noise is filtered from your voice to register any questions or commands you have for Alexa.

The Echo comes with a grille on the bottom half of the device with a ring LED on the top edge. A mute button is available to switch off the otherwise ever-listening microphones (if you ever want a little bit of privacy), as shown in the above picture and an "action" button which can be used to manually tell it to perform a specific task. This button is also used to initiate the setup process of the Echo.

The remote control included is an extra tool if you ever find yourself too far from Alexa to hear you, or if you find yourself in a situation where you're stuck and can't move to tell Alexa something (hmm… sitting on the toilet perhaps?).

The ring of light gives it a fine futuristic touch. During the initial setup it illuminates an orange glow as well as every time you use the trigger word, 'Alexa' or provide a specific command. When you change the volume the ring of light will turn white, the length which the light glows around the ring of the Echo represents the volume level. The ring twists either left or right in order to control the volume, which can also be done with the remote.

There is a classic gray Amazon logo at the bottom of the speaker and the top half is entirely unembellished, apart from the volume ring.

The Echo is otherwise a modest device when it comes to judging it by its appearance but it has a myriad of impressive properties underneath the facade. The matte black finish is quick to accumulate oil from fingers and will leave prints all over the body which provides you the incentive to go hands free by maximizing the feature of voice recognition, just as the Echo was designed for.

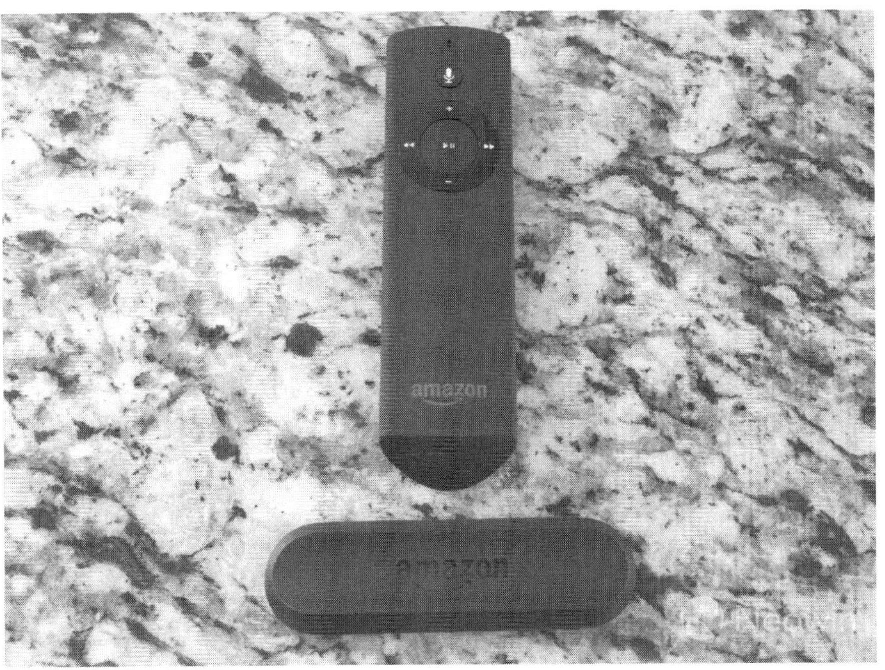
amazon
amazon

CHAPTER 4 – WHAT HAVE THEY ALL BEEN SAYING ABOUT ALEXA AND THE ECHO?

Since the availability of the nine and a quarter inch tall black compact cylinder to a larger public, a number of reviews have been released to assess everything that the Echo is and all the functionalities it has to offer. Almost over 90% of the users and expert reviews have given positive feedback to the attributes of this new household technology.

The Executive Editor of *TechHive* Mr. Michael Brown says, “Amazon’s Echo is the best voice-controlled product that I’ve seen at the consumer level. It’s versatile, powerful, and amazingly quick to recognize your speech and then do something.”

The design of the Bluetooth speaker is attractively compact and durable. "This is a speaker you can fit anywhere in your home. And because it weighs around 700g, you don't have to worry about it being easily knocked over by small children or animals. It's a solid, weighty thing that squeezes into a range of spaces – whether that be a table top, kitchen counter or nestled by your living room's entertainment center," explains Elyse Betters, the technology report expert of *Pocket-lint.*

A lot of the reviewers find that the most interesting feature the Amazon Echo has is the enjoyment it offers after responding to their voice. The moment Alexa responds to your voice, it would take just a few exchanges for you to get hooked.

"When it first arrived I was wowed by how well the Echo worked," says Stacey Higginbotham of the *Fortune.* The sassy voice of Alexa will be a constant source of entertainment as well as being a handy tool in the house. "We think hands-free voice control is a godsend and that Alexa, Amazon Echo's personal assistant, truly distinguishes this Bluetooth speaker from the competition. It blew our minds. We won't ever get tired of walking into our living room and casually asking Alexa..," adds Elysse Betters.

Alexa does have a way of catching the attention of any member of the family, a statement that Executive Editor of *CNET* Mr. David Carnoy agrees with after saying the following about Echo in one of his reviews posted online "Echo…is a likeable device that seems to grow on people over time as it continues to improve." The moment Alexa captivates your attention, you will find it harder and harder to resist her charms as you get to know her more and more.

The Echo is probably the first in the list of Intelligent Personal Assistants that was created solely for use in the convenience of the user's home. *Gizmag*'s Eric Mack agrees that "there's truly nothing else out there right now just like it". Alexa responds with remarkably relatively lesser time delays, as compared with other intelligent personal assistants that come with smart phones, and with a simulated voice that is close to being almost human.

One impressive advantage Alexa has as an Intelligent Personal Assistant lies in its seven strategically located powerful and sensitive microphones to pick up the sound of your voice. Mr. Mack has been markedly impressed with this feature, saying that "you'll be pleasantly surprised by Echo's ability to hear and understand just about any voice right out of the box without training (although the training is recommended to improve the software, it's light years beyond smaller devices with fewer microphones). Most impressive is Echo's ability to hear commands even when it's playing music at maximum volume."

'I never found it necessary to speak in overly simplistic phrases or even to speak slowly. In fact, I was stunned by how fast I could speak and still have the Echo recognize my sentences—even when I uttered them while it was playing music or responding to an earlier question or instruction," *TechHive's* Mr. Brown adds.

Alexa is indeed attentive to your voice and a very good listener who is always all ears twenty four hours a day, seven days a week. This prominent attribute is indeed a definite plus for the Echo, especially for those who have experienced using voice prompted software that frustratingly never seem to get a single word right, or at times do not even seem to hear you at all. Having to repeat what you say is not only a waste of time and effort, but can also be excruciatingly irritating.

The practicality of having Alexa in the household for a cascade of simple inquiries and to organize schedules, or to update a to-do list and even to control household lights and other devices, is part of the reasons why it may prove to be indispensable.

Being called just a "smart" home device does not give enough justice to the Echo's attribute of being able to constantly learn from its humans, as well as learn from its developers who instantly feed her the most recent updates available in the internet. This updating takes place even while the Echo is busy with other affairs in the household. Often Echo would simply surprise its users with upgraded new functionalities and new tricks and treats for them to try.

"That's what makes me the most excited about the Echo. It's already an amazing, intelligent music player today, but it also has the potential to evolve into the hub for everything electronic in my home," exclaims personal investor Jeff Bezos of the *Business Insider.*

Users have gotten used to having the Amazon Echo in the house as Alexa has become an integral part of their household. Nick Pino of *TechRadar* shares how the Echo has imbedded itself into their lives, "After spending a week with it in my home, it's clear that Amazon Echo is something you don't know you want until you have it, and something you don't miss until it's gone."

With the great pool of reviews and secondary source information available you can probably see more clearly that the Amazon Echo lives up to what it claims. Stacey Higginbotham of the *Fortune* nailed it, "The Amazon Echo is one of the few connected devices that work as advertised. And it's only getting better." "The Echo is a powerful and very well designed product with a bright future. Good job, Amazon," adds Mr. Michael Brown of *TechHive.*

By now you are probably excited to meet Alexa, hang on to your nose because in the next chapter I will help set you up with the girl that has captured the hearts, and minds, of a number of people within a span of less than a year from her release.

CHAPTER 5 - SET ME UP WITH ALEXA!

Setting up the Amazon Echo and resetting it is about as easy as anyone could ask for. The moment it's plugged in, it instantaneously takes-off into ready mode by acting as an access point for Wi-Fi. With the use of a tablet or a smart phone, all you have to do is momentarily make a connection to the Echo through Wi-Fi and you're off!

Alexa will tell you the moment the connection is successful, and direct you in using the Echo app (which should have already been installed ahead of time on your tablet or smart phone) to complete this part of the set-up process.

From there, all you need to do is tell the Echo which Wi-Fi router it should make a connection to and then feed it the Wi-Fi security/password code. The Echo app will then prompt you to check out an orientation video, however, if you want to skip ahead, you can just skip to the end and the Echo app will give you a chance to move on. The introductory video played by the app, is just a walkthrough of a few basic voice commands to assist in ensuring you're fully up and running

In short, all you need to do is three simple steps:

1. **Plug in the Echo**
2. **Download the Echo app**
3. **Follow the instructions from the app**

This Echo app is available for Amazon Fire phones and tablets as well as Apple and Android devices. However, it's also possible to access the app through your computer by connecting from a web browser (type in echo.amazon.com).

After you give the Amazon Echo access to a Wi-Fi network (which is how it gains a connection to the cloud services and automatically upgrades or streams music), it will be up and running very shortly in a few mere minutes. One awesome thing with the setup is that you don't actually need to manually setup your Echo (unless you consider plugging a cable into the socket as manual labor!), once it gains a connection to the cloud services and hooks into your Wi-Fi network, it's good to go!

After you're set up, you can begin talking to Alexa. Alexa's voice sounds less robotic than Siri, but it isn't exactly human either which is good in a sense. Would you really want a technological device sounding like a real human…?

I didn't think so!

Currently it's not possible to change the voice in the configuration settings but then again it's highly unlikely it will stay this way in the near future as other options will be provided.

The Amazon Echo makes use of an on-device keyword spotting that enables it to detect a wake word, therefore the moment you say "Alexa," the light instantaneously turns on and the Amazon Echo springs into action. If for any reason the name "Alexa" isn't convenient within your house, you can change the wake word to "Amazon" through the settings. In the app, go to Settings, select your Amazon Echo, and then select **Wake Word**. It is possible in the near future that you will be able to customize and select your own Wake Word once Amazon implements this feature.

Out of the box, the voice recognition of the Echo is pretty amazing. You won't have any trouble with your words being misunderstood by Alexa. In fact, voice services will get even better with time as you use it, especially since the Echo makes use of your own voice recordings in order to improve its results. On the other hand, you can improve this with the help of the Voice Training that is found in the Echo app if you wish.

With the voice recognition, there is a lot that you can enjoy doing with the Amazon Echo as it grants you the ability to ask questions about the news, sports and weather and get up to date answers, set alarms and stream music online simply by talking. In addition to that, the Amazon Echo can assist you with items for your shopping and to-do lists. Depending on what you prefer, you can add items to the lists either through your voice or by manually inputting them. However, you can currently only take out the lists through the app which isn't much of an issue as the app is user-friendly.

Each and every command starts with the wake word

"Alexa," and you don't have to wait for Echo to acknowledge herself in order to complete your command (i.e., just saying, "Alexa, what's the time?" works well enough.) The default listening mode of Echo is always on, just like the "Hey Siri" feature of the iPhone. Nevertheless, you can manually switch off the Echo's continuous listening, and you will still be able give voice commands through the remote control microphone if you wish.

In the first few weeks of June 2015, Amazon has yet again treated its Echo users with excessive indulgence by adding a new feature into the device. Now you can have Alexa read your audio books to you through your Amazon Audible books subscription. Audible books is an Amazon subordinate company that hosts over a hundred and fifty thousand literary works recorded in audio. It is the most comprehensive audio book and recorded literary work provider all throughout the world. All you have to do is navigate through the Amazon Echo or the Echo application on your tablet or smart phones so you can start playing your audio books, pause it, or ask Alexa to move either forward or backwards in the audiobook. Or you can simply call out to Alexa with a simple, "Alexa, read *The*

Secret Garden". Whisper sync for Voice app works as a virtual bookmark for Echo that would allow you to pick up from where you last stopped on a title you have on either on a Kindle reading app or Audible app. So when you are interrupted while in the middle of listening to your audio book, you can just call out "Alexa, pause" and then once you are ready call out for Alexa to "resume" your book.

In much the same time, Amazon has also found a way to better help you with organizing daily schedules. By linking Google calendars to your Amazon Echo interface, Alexa can now call out events from your calendar or inform you about important events of the day such as holidays and birthdays. With this new feature, it is now easier for you to manage and never forget your scheduled tasks. Simply let Alexa jog your memory by reading out events from your calendar.

Updating the Echo's software has also activated its ability to employ the actual traffic information in your place in order to advise you with the best routes to take as well as the estimated time of your travel. Travelling? No problem. Wake up Alexa and ask for the best route towards your destination.

Recently, Amazon added Belkini WeMo and Philips Hue integration, which is an exceptional update. WeMo and Hue support provides you an opportunity to control compatible gadgets and devices within the house with very simple commands such as; "Alexa, turn on the kitchen light." This of course is only currently compatible with WeMo or Hue products. Fortunately enough, it works with most Hue products, meaning that you can control your Hue Lux bulbs without any glitches. On the other hand, currently the Echo is only able to work with a few of the WeMo devices. These include the Switch, Insight Switch and the Light Switch. All these featured products of Hue and WeMo are on sale at Amazon. Stay tuned and soon enough you'll be able to clap your hands to turn the lights on and off!

CHAPTER 6 – ALEXA, I'D LOVE TO HAVE DINNER BUT THAT DATE DOESN'T WORK FOR ME!

To change your Amazon shipping date for the Amazon Echo, please follow the steps outlined below:

- Sign in to your Amazon account and locate your order
- Select the 'Change Shipping Speed' option
- From there, click on the option, 'Select Another Date and Time'
- Chose another date and time which works for you from the calendar
- After that, click 'Confirm' and you're done

Note:

If your Amazon Echo has already been shipped, or you didn't make a schedule of the date and time of delivery, then you can't change your shipping date. You will have to contact customer support on Amazon to find out alternative options.

Also, once you have placed an order, you can edit the date of delivery of your subscriptions under the 'Your Subscribe and Save Items' tab through the following simple steps:

- After you go to the 'Your Subscribed and Save Items' menu, select 'Edit Delivery Date' alongside the date of your monthly delivery
- Select your new date of delivery using the calendar
- After that, select confirm and you are good to go.

Note:

The moment you edit the monthly 'Subscribe and Save'

date of delivery, all your active subscriptions change to the date of arrival for the address that is associated with the named subscriptions. In addition, you can also move the deliveries of future subscriptions to the dates of your upcoming deliveries by selecting the 'Move to' option.

CHAPTER 7 – ALEXA, YOU'RE SUCH A BOOKWORM

When it comes to information, you can find out a lot from Alexa. Any answer that Alexa has given you for questions that you've asked, or any song she's played will all be recorded, stored and accessible on the Echo app. This provides you with an opportunity to reflect on all the questions you have previously asked giving you the option to dig deeper for more information through sources such as Wikipedia or Google if you wish.

Alexa has no trouble telling you the weather forecast for the day, or weekend for the city that you are currently in (or soon to be visiting). This includes the weather forecast for a multitude of cities worldwide. As mentioned, you're not required to wait for Alexa to catch up once you've called her; you simply say "Alexa, what's the weather?" and you are immediately provided an answer such as:

"Right now, in New Jersey its 75 degrees with clear skies and sun. Today's weather forecast is mostly sunny, with a high of 78 and a low of 64."

Other things Alexa is capable of doing includes: word definitions, state capitals, holiday dates and measurements (i.e. how many tablespoons are in a cup), sports news inquiry, reading out your Google calendar and traffic advisory.

The Echo is able to automatically hook into Wikipedia; therefore, you can receive spoken information on essentially anything. However, the only string attached is that you have to get used to saying "**Alexa, Wikipedia: Horsepower**" instead of "Alexa, what is Horsepower?"

In case you're looking for overall info on a particular person, thing, event, or place, you can simply ask your Amazon Echo to continue reading the first paragraph of an article from Wikipedia. If you want to instruct Echo to read an excerpt of a Wikipedia article, say:

"Alexa, Wikipedia: Strawberry."

Alexa will read out the opening paragraph of the specific article and then include a link to the article in the Echo App.

TIP: Amazon Echo will not read the complete article, nevertheless, you can say "More”, "Tell me more" or “Hear More” in order to have Alexa read you more info from the article off Wikipedia.

Here are a few more ways of getting information from Alexa:

If you want to know more about people, you can ask,

"Alexa, who is {name}?"

"Alexa, who is {position}?"

If you have an interest in knowing what happened or happens on a particular date, or when a certain event happened:

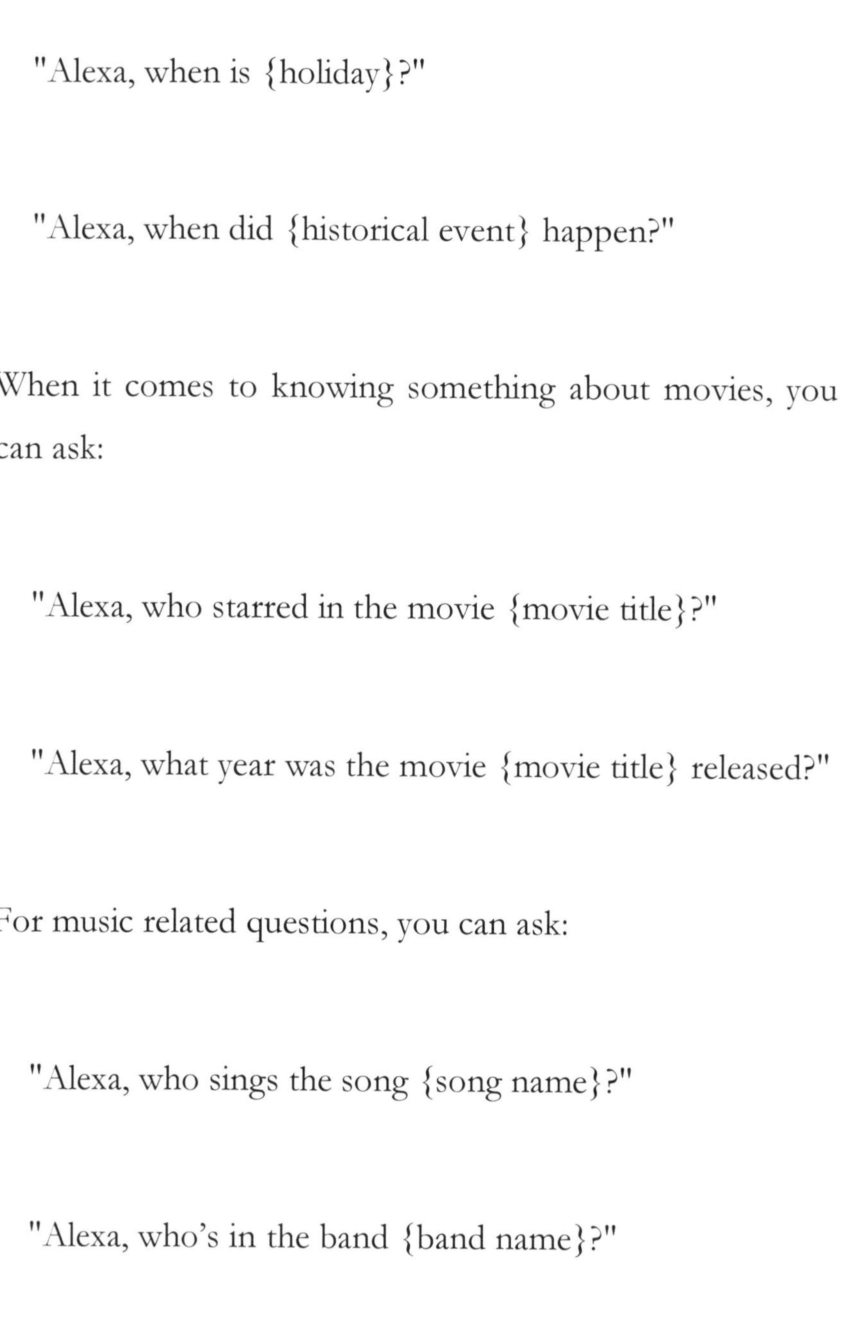

"Alexa, when is {holiday}?"

"Alexa, when did {historical event} happen?"

When it comes to knowing something about movies, you can ask:

"Alexa, who starred in the movie {movie title}?"

"Alexa, what year was the movie {movie title} released?"

For music related questions, you can ask:

"Alexa, who sings the song {song name}?"

"Alexa, who's in the band {band name}?"

"Alexa, what year did {band name} release {album title or song title}?"

Educative questions can also be well answered by Alexa, for instance; to ask about the spelling of a word, you say,

"Alexa, how do you spell {word}?"

Definitions can also be answered by Alexa by simply asking:

“Alexa, what is the definition of {word}?"

If you want the answer to a unit conversion:

"Alexa, how many {units} are in a {units}?"

Or you can phrase it like this,

"Alexa, how many {units} are in {number} {units}?"

Mathematical operations such as: addition, subtraction, multiplication, division, square roots, factorial and power operations can also be solved by Alexa. However, Alexa can only accept a single mathematical operation in every question, for example, 11 + 7 or 17 x 6. Calculations such as 2 + 4 + 8 or (7-5) x 32 are not currently supported.

Geographical questions are easily answered by the Echo. These are examples of questions you could ask in this regard:

"Alexa, what is the distance between {location} and {location}?"

"Alexa, what is the capital city of {location}?"

"Alexa, what is the latitude and longitude of {location}?"

"Alexa, what is the elevation of {location}?"

"Alexa, which {countries or states} border {location}?"

If you're a sports enthusiast Alexa won't let you down! You can ask about NBA games, as well as NFL, MLB, MLS, and NHL games. Examples of sports questions that Alexa can answer are…

Scores for a certain game...

"Alexa, what was the score of the {sports team} game?"

"Alexa, did the {sports team} win?"

Information about live games can also be retrieved from the Echo, you can get it by asking;

"Alexa, who is winning the {sports team} game?"

The Echo can also provide you with information about any games that are upcoming, all you have to do is ask!

"Alexa, when do the {sports team} play next?" or

"Alexa, when is the next {sports team} game?"

Information for general knowledge is also easily retrieved from Amazon Echo, for example you can ask about the local time of a specific city in the world,

"Alexa, what time is it in {city}?"

The nutritional information about a specific food can be retrieved from Alexa,

"Alexa, how many calories are there in {food item}?

By linking your Google account to your Amazon Echo, you are now able to ask Alexa about your schedules and dates of any particular event listed in your calendar. A question that goes:

"Alexa, what's my schedule today?"

Can result to an answer that goes this way:

"On John's calendar, there is one event. There is work, which lasts from 8 AM to 5 PM."

You can ask Alexa to summarize your schedule for you, or ask her about your schedule on a particular date as well as the date of a particular event, but actually inputting a schedule using Alexa alone is currently not yet supported. You can do this by modifying your Google calendars, though.

You can keep experimenting with a lot more questions to find out how far you can stretch this smart beauty, and over time Amazon will refine the potential of questions even further and expand upon them.

CHAPTER 8 – ALEXA ARE YOU CHEATING ON ME WITH ECHO APP?

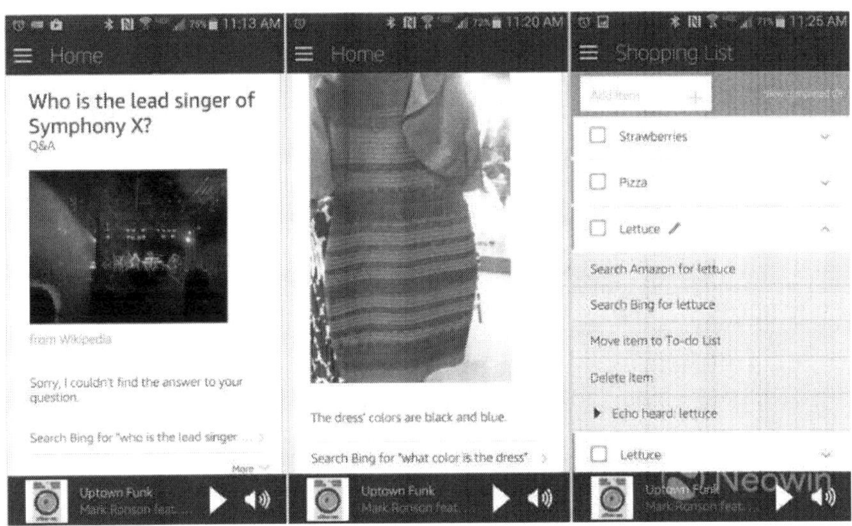

The Echo app can be used in lieu of the voice input in order to interact with the Echo. It has the ability to gain access to all your to-do lists, the alarm functions, the timer, and handle all the linked online music services that you've paired Alexa with. The app can suggest things to try with

Alexa, and also serves as a media player that has the controls for the tower.

The Echo app itself comes with a home screen which defaults to the most recent queries and commands that you've given Alexa. There is also an Echo card that shows the most common controls that you have used as well as the specific options which depend on your most frequent interaction, these include:

- A brief description of what was played or what was requested
- Some options for browsing similar content that is found within the app
- Links for you to find more information
- Feedback options for voice commands and ways of improving your voice recognition
- An option to remove this card

A tab that is located in the upper-left corner of the app slides out to reveal a variety of options that are sub-divided into three categories. You can easily access your shopping and to-do lists at the top. In addition, you can set timers and alarms that will sound through the Echo at the appropriate times.

Further down the list you can gain immediate access to your music options such as Amazon Prime Music, Spotify, TuneIn, Pandora, iTunes and iHeartRadio. If no streaming service has been specified, the Echo app will default to Prime Music.

You can also link to the Amazon Echo via Bluetooth to use it as a traditional speaker and play any local content off your device that is connected via Bluetooth.

The Echo app much like the cylindrical Amazon Echo hardware is lacking all the fancy embellishment and ornamentation, instead Amazon has chosen to keep it to the minimal with simple interfaces and a straightforward and easy to use platform. The home screen readily directs you to the commands and queries you have thrown at Alexa in the immediate past, with presentation of the most recent tasks to the oldest.

A sliding tab in the upper left corner of the screen provides options you can work with when working with the app. The options are further divided into subcategories. Your shopping and To-do lists, along with the times and alarms you have set up, are easily accessible at the top of the screen. At the bottom of these options, you will find your music selection and workable features. And further below, near the bottom of the screen, are practical options such as Help, Settings, Voice Training and Recommendations for things to try.

CHAPTER 9 - TIPS AND TRICKS ALEXA CAN PERFORM

Here are a variety of tips and tricks that enables you to use Alexa to her fullest potential. These tips and tricks cover the areas of:

Music

Upload your own Music: The Amazon Echo doesn't provide the opportunity to input SD cards or utilize other similar music and data storage devices for your songs. On the flip side, you're allowed to upload up to 250 songs for free to the Amazon Cloud Player. All you have to do is go to the Amazon Cloud Player from your Amazon account and start uploading immediately. After that, Alexa will gladly play your requests.

Amazon Prime Music: If you're a Prime Subscriber, you will be able to access the music library from Amazon Prime. Just ask Alexa to play a specific song or an artist from the immense library of Prime Music that is available to listen to.

"Alexa, play some Madonna."

Alexa can now also stream ad-free music stations with your pre-defined playlists. Prime Stations from the Prime Music allows you to skip through your music as often as you want, pause playing in the middle of a song, turn the volume up or down and all other basic audio media playing operations you can think of. You can even give the song a thumbs up or a thumbs down to let Echo know which songs you prefer listening to. This will let Alexa know what songs you prefer and the ones you don't, so that the next time you ask her to play music she can play the ones that you like. To make things even more exciting, the more you use Alexa the more she learns from your choices. So in a manner of speaking, the more you spend time with your girl, the moments you share with her gets more and more enjoyable.

Listen to Pandora: The Amazon Echo is also capable of doing all these with the Pandora music platform. Simply link your Pandora account to the Echo and you are geared up to enjoy your most convenient, high tech listening experience ever. And since Echo is always listening, always alert and always connected to the cloud, any modifications you ask Alexa to do such as creating new stations and or editing your playlist through the Echo application will be applied to your music account. With this, you will be able to listen to your improved music stations anywhere and anytime you are on the go.

Note: This feature can only be enjoyed if you have updated your Amazon Echo Echo app to the latest version that can handle these new features.

Stream in music from TuneIn and iHeartRadio: As if the Pandora, Amazon Music and Prime Music are not enough to help you get lost into your music euphoria, the geeks and skillful experts of the Amazon lab just have to coddle you with more options. Now you can stream your music from iHeartRadio and TuneIn. With a mere verbal request, you can ask Alexa to play any song you want under any streaming radio of your pick.

Play through Bluetooth: Also, let us not forget that the Amazon Echo is first and foremost a smart Bluetooth speaker. If you get tired of playing with the built in support Echo offers for the above programs, you can always play any audio you have available in your phones or tablets. Unlike other Bluetooth speakers, there is a woofer and a tweeter imbedded in the Echo's cylindrical frame. These technical parts make sure the bass and treble of your sounds are adjusted just right so you can enjoy superior quality audio every time. Having the speaker release sound in 360 degrees guarantees that you will be able to hear the Amazon Echo from any portion of the room without much distortion.

Traffic

Traffic updates: Alexa can now inform you of the easiest and fastest route to work taking into account any traffic jams, road works or car accidents that have occurred on your normal route to work. All you'll need to do is simply go to the echo.amazon.com site to set up your home and work addresses.

To get Alexa to do this for you, you must first go into the Echo app and plug in information on your starting point and your destination location. Then you can ask Alexa about traffic between the two locations, you can say, "Alexa, how is traffic?"

Information about alternate routes along with their travel times can also be asked from Alexa. Aside from hearing Alexa speak aloud these details, you can also view them on screen using your Echo app.

All the traffic navigation is conducted by a Nokia company called HERE which is a huge location cloud set up for use anywhere in the world. HERE has linked together an all-encompassing range of software and hardware which has the capacity of providing location services. And with this broad range of service, it is able to provide quality locating service to anyone connected to the cloud.

Weather

Ask for local, national and international weather predictions: All it takes is for you to indicate where you have set up the Amazon Echo, input your zip code and you are all hooked up to begin asking Alexa about weather conditions.

You can learn the current weather condition in your local area, in another state in the U.S. or a city anywhere else in the world. The information Alexa provides can be highly reliable based on updates from AccuWeather every 30 minutes.

You can even find out weather conditions for any location for up to seven days in advance. Just give a shout out to Alexa and you don't ever have to worry about wearing the wrong outfit or leaving the house without your umbrella. After each weather request for any location, a page would pop out of the Echo app with details on the 7 day forecast for that particular location.

Snowfall amounts: Currently, Alexa isn't able to provide amounts of snowfall, however don't expect that to be for much longer!

If you ask "Alexa, will it snow today?" or "Alexa, will it snow on Monday?" she will provide you with the likelihood of snow as well as the probable amount. This will also be true to asking Alexa for the likelihood of rain for the day.

Shopping

Managing your Shopping List: Adding items to your shopping list or to-do list is as easy as asking a real life personal assisant to physically input these items into a sheet of paper. The advantage of having Alexa do it for you instead is you don't even have to fumble over pen and paper and you are sure you can easily access this list because the moment you tell Alexa the things you need it gets instantly uploaded and stored into the cloud.

If you want to double check on your latest list ask Alexa to run it through with you. Just say, "Alexa, what's on my Shopping List?" or "Alexa, what's on my To-do list?"

The Echo app will allow you to re-examine up to a hundred items on your Shopping or To-do lists. Add and delete items on your list by acceessing the Echo app and view the items or activities you have checked off your list.

Printing off your Shopping List: Alexa doesn't currently print on command sadly, nonetheless you can go over to the echo.amazon.com site on your personal computer and from their website you will be able to print out your shopping or to-do lists. As an alternative, you can use third-party printer apps that is connected to your Amazon Echo via the IFTTT (this exciting new feature deserves a separate chapter and details about its use and functionality is elaborated in that chapter). However, in order to use this function, your printer must have a compatible application "channel" in the IFTTT website. In other words, if your printer does not have the application required to connect it to your Echo, then you still will not be able to print out your lists using Echo alone.

Using Amazon to shop: You can shop on the Echo app to search for things you want to purchase through Amazon or Bing. This works in much the same way as you ordinarily browse through items on the online websites.

Reorder supplies in your home: The Amazon has finally been equipped with the capability of doing voice-directed shopping through a built-in coded instruction that allows you to re-order items you have already ordered recently. Take note, you should have already purchased these items previously. If you ask Alexa to look over things that you have not yet had delivered on your doorstep, Amazon Echo will give you its best association for the item along with its price. If you still are not satisfied with what Alexa has provided you, she will keep the item on your shopping list and wait for you to make purchase decisions yourself by the time you get a hold of your phone, tablet, computer or any device capable with a browser.

To have Alexa resupply your household kitchen towels, for example, all you have to do is say, "Alexa, reorder kitchen towels."

Amazon will then try to locate the past purchases you have transacted using the Amazon account you have Echo registered with. Alexa will tell you the occurring price of the item, for this case the present price of a kitchen towel you have recently bought on Amazon, then confirm if you want to proceed with the purchase.

If for instance you have not yet purchased kitchen towels using your Amazon account and the Echo does not find any details about it in your order history, it will instantly provide you with a suggestion based on its "Amazon's choice."

> "I didn't find that in your order history, but Amazon's Choice for kitchen towel is Liliane Collection Kitchen Dish Towels (13 Units) – Commercial Grade Absorbent 100% Cotton Kitchen Towels (Size 25" x 14") – Classic Tea Towels in White with Blue Stripes – Bakers Dozen Includes 13 Kitchen Towels by Liliane Collection. The order total is $14.99. Should I order it?"

If you choose to proceed with Amazon's Choice then simply give Alexa a "Yes", if not, Alexa will add the item to your Shopping List. You can then continue with the purchase of the item using the Echo app.

You also don't need to worry about committing mistakes while instructing Alexa for a purchase order. Shout out "Alexa, cancel order" and the last item you asked for to be purchased will be canceled. Easy.

The Amazon Echo places these orders using your default payment and shipping details specified in your Amazon account. And since it is all managed by Amazon, all your orders are also eligible for free returns as long as it keeps within the company's return policy.

Tip: To insure yourself with additional security for this Amazon Echo feature, you can put in a verbal confirmation code using the Echo app. Or alternatively if you find this security measure too risky, you can just connect to the Echo app and turn off purchasing via voice prompts.

But wait, there's more. The catch behind this feature is that the capability is restricted only for users who have Prime subscriptions under Amazon. The items for order must also be qualified for Prime shipping with both a recognized United States billing address and a United States recognized mode of payment.

Purchase Songs: Now you can purchase songs with just a voice command through the Amazon Echo. The Echo has already been programmed to allow you to buy music from Amazon's very own Digital Music Store. Can you imagine how luxuriously convenient this act is? Form an image in your mind of you pleasantly enjoying an online radio station played through the Echo and then suddenly you stumble upon a new song you want to buy. You can ask

Alexa to give the title of this song and then ask her to make the purchase for you.

In order to do this, you must first make sure that you have activated voice purchasing on the Echo app and added the 1-Click payment method as well. Billing address should be in the United States and the 1-Click payment method issued by a U.S. bank. Using Amazon Gift Cards for purchase is also available on Echo, just make sure you are presently residing in the United States.

To purchase a song or album just say this:

"Alexa, shop for the song I Just Haven't Met You Yet"

"Alexa, shop for the album 1989"

Or you can shop for a song by artist:

"Alexa, shop for (new) songs by Celine Dion"

If you are not yet sure with what to purchase you can ask Alexa for suggestions:

"Alexa, what is popular with Michael Buble?"

Then to buy it, you can say:

"Alexa, buy this song"

"Alexa, buy this album"

All your music purchases are stored in your Amazon account's Music library with no additional costs. If another person in the household wants to purchase a song but would like it into his or her own personal account, simply tell Alexa the following:

"Alexa, switch accounts"

Then proceed with buying the song in the currently active account.

Wikipedia

Asking simple questions: For general information off the Wikipedia online encyclopedia, you can ask Alexa anything about a specific place, dates, event, person, thing and she will read out the first paragraph written about the topic on the Wikipedia article. All it takes is an:

"Alexa, Wikipedia: _______"

If you want to hear Alexa read more about the article just ask her to tell you "More."

You can ask any particular question, but please note that the Amazon Echo may not be able to have answers for everything. This is not a problem, just let the experts in the Amazon lab know about this and be assured they will do something about this.

Guessing the age of a celebrity: Have you ever wondered how old a famous actor, actress or celebrity is while watching your favorite TV Shows? You can know a celebrity's age by just asking Alexa! For instance, give her a shout and ask:

"Alexa, how old is Scarlet Johansson?"

Asking about movies and music information: In the middle of a conversation with a friend, or while listening to your station using the Amazon Echo you can give a shout out to Alexa to ask her a few entertainment new questions:

> "Alexa, who starred in the movie _________?"
>
> "Alexa, in what year did the movie __________ come out?"
>
> "Alexa, who sings the song _______?"
>
> "Alexa, who is in the band _______?"
>
> "Alexa, what year did ________ release _______?"

Knowledge enhancing questions: Alexa can spell words, give English definitions, and convert different units of measurement. You may find all these features very useful inside the house, especially if you are raising young kids. Anyone who has spent time with a toddler or primary school kid for at least 2 hours can say that these little ones are truly naturally inquisitive. Anyone has, at a point in their lives, probably experienced being stuck with a kid loaded with simple and interesting questions. You start out okay, you are able to answer most of the start-up questions and often you even encourage it, but then comes the second question, followed by the next, and then another one, and another one, and then you reach the point when you get tired and feel drained and you can't seem to answer the question anymore. The kid seems tireless. Well, Alexa can help you out in this situation. Just instruct the kid to ask away and Alexa would, as she always does, answer the curious little bunny's questions for you. And if Alexa don't have the answers to some of the kid's questions, don't worry too much the kid can leave with it and he or she can just move on to his or her next question. No worries.

In the event that Alexa is filled with so much information that words can't seem to express it efficiently with the use of words, she will direct your attention to her dependable partner the Amazon Echo app. Talk about opportune comfort and convenience.

Audible

We have seen that Alexa can keep your shopping and To-do lists, she can play your music, purchase supplies for you and answer a number of your questions. But now, Alexa can also read books for you. Think of her as your personal bedtime or tea time storyteller.

Alexa can access your Audible account and read books you have available upon voice command. This feature is included in Amazon Echo's latest update and has been much awaited by Echo users.

Calendars

Once you have set up the Echo with Google, Alexa can now update you with your calendar details, consequently anyone else present in the house can also gain access to your schedule. In the event that you have a couple or more calendars, you can take charge of which calendar you want Echo to gain access to by managing it on the Echo app. However, without specifying this detail on the app the Amazon Echo will not distinguish between your calendars and instead provide you details coming from *all* your calendars. To some this may be useful, but for others it may prove to be counterproductive.

Currently, it is not yet possible for any other member of the family to link their own personal Google calendar accounts with the Echo. Only one personal Google calendar can be supported by the Amazon Echo, as of the moment.

Here are a few of the questions you can shoot at Alexa that concerns the use of your Google calendar.

You can ask Alexa for the next event on your schedule with:

"Alexa, when is my next event?"

Or you can have her summarize everything you have planned out for the day.

"Alexa, what's on my calendar?"

You can ask Alexa what you have planned for another date:

"Alexa, what's on my calendar on Saturday?"

Or a specific event you jotted down at a particular time on a different date:

"Alexa, what's on my calendar tomorrow at 9 PM?"

Setup

Reconfiguration of your Wi-Fi: If you recently changed the password of your Wi-Fi, and Alexa starts giving you the silent treatment, you'll need to press and hold the "Action" button for roughly 5 seconds. The color of the light ring will turn orange, and from there, you can make use of the Amazon Echo app on your mobile device to reconfigure the Echo Wi-Fi password to the updated password.

Voice Training: Treat Alexa as if she is a young child you have just recently brought into the family. Like a child, she still has a lot to learn and needs to master skills that would make her function more efficiently. Alexa learns by listening more to your voice and adjusting to your schedules, habits, and routines. She learns well with constant practice and with frequent repetitions she learns to adapt to the new environment. As she cozies up into your home, she adds more into her skills and in return provides better quality service.

Voice training will be able to aid the Amazon Echo to

easily detect and understand the words you speak to her. This practice is done so that the Echo will be better able to distinguish the phrases and requests you deliver.

Amazon will instruct you through the voice training process and it is highly recommended that you follow the following requirements before proceeding with the training. First, make sure that the microphones are properly functioning before proceeding with the drill. You will be able to determine if the device is off if the light on top of Echo's edges lights up red. Just press the microphone power button to enable the use of the microphones. Next, situate yourself in a location from where you would normally be whenever you talk to Alexa. You may choose to either stand, sit, crouch, squat, lay down or whatever suits you but just make sure that your distance from the Echo is about the same distance you normally would be from the Echo during ordinary occasions.

Remember to speak in your normal voice, with the usual speed, volume, intonation and pronunciation. You are training Alexa to adjust to your voice and not the other way around. Also try to avoid intentionally confusing Alexa during the training period. Also, do not use the remote control device during the voice training. This will only defeat the purpose of the training because Alexa will then be adjusting to the sound of your voice fed through the remote control's microphone instead of to your voice as heard during normal situations when you are across the room and your voice is exposed with background interferences that causes distortions. What the Amazon Echo is training for in this practice is to be able to adjust to the sound of your speaking voice when you are in the room talking to her without the use of the remote control device. After checking that all the conditions are in order, you can now proceed with the voice training.

Voice training can be done by first opening the Echo app and selecting the "Voice Training" action. Once you hit the start button, you will be asked to read a total of twenty five different phrases in your normal speaking voice. You will be asked to read the phrases one at a time. When you want to repeat a phrase you have just read, just select "Pause" and then select "Repeat phase". Once your session has ended you can go back to the home page of your Echo app. If on the other hand you want to end your session while still in the middle of the session, just select "Pause" and then "End session"

Viewing your Dialog History: One of the Amazon Echo's useful attributes is the ability to provide you with the best options and recommendations that suite your unique preference by learning from all your inputs. As a human being gets to know another human being, in the same manner the Amazon Echo gets to know you more by finding out your personality and preference through your requests, commands, and recent activities. In order to do this, the Amazon Echo must keep a record of all your communications. You may refer to these recordings as her notes and records that account for her entire life's worth of study.

To listen and view all the conversations you have shared with Alexa, you can simply go to the "Dialog History" under the "Settings" options of your Echo app. To delete individual voice recordings you can select "Delete voice recordings" in the same page where your dialog history is located. Deleting all the recorded transactions you have shared with Alexa, you have to access your Amazon Echo account and go to the "Your

Devices" section, select your Amazon Echo from your account and open the "Device Actions", select "Manage Recordings" and hit "Delete".

You may find this option more self-comforting, placing your mind at ease and lessening on the paranoiac tendencies. But deleting all your recordings means that everything Alexa has been working on will be deleted. You have burned all her notes and may have to start from scratch once again. This means she needs to learn more about you once again in order to provide you with more relevant suggestions. This is like enjoying a date with a tech savvy girl. You enjoyed your date from the moment you laid eyes on her until the last moment when you said goodbye to her in front of the porch of her house. You talked a lot and shared a lot of information about each other, with you doing much of the talking. She found out a lot about you and was very attentive to every word you say, giving responses whenever you asked her. Everything would have been great, but the next time you meet her for another date, you found out that she has lost all of her memory about you. In order for her to know you, you must repeat everything you told her and start from the beginning. This is a simple analogy of what happens when you erase all your Echo's contents.

Listening to the recordings and to the sound of your voice may be a bit creepy. It's even doubly creepy that there is an option of being able to read a transcribed copy of all your communications with Alexa.

A few consumers have shunned the Amazon Echo because of this feature. Many have argued that this feature may make the Echo very unsafe and risky. They feel that in the hands of the wrong people, these may be used to invade on their personal lives. Also, the privacy issue can be a bit of a controversy. Techie paranoid individuals are just so afraid that Amazon lab geeks may have access to these recordings and compromise individual privacy rights.

Although in Echo's defense, Amazon has blatantly stated to the public that they should not fear the device because for as long as they are concerned, these conversations do not reach them and are entirely shared just between the Echo and you.

Other features

Use the remote to say "Simon Says": Alexa is such a limelight hoarder that it is understandably easy to forget about the accessory remote control device that comes with your purchase of the Amazon Echo. With the little functionality the remote control device holds and not to mention its utter devotion to the star Alexa, it is understandably easy how we can just as readily take the device for granted during the first weeks of having the Echo package in the house. But let us not forget that there are situations when we may actually find the use of the remote control device to be more convenient than simply talking directly to Alexa.

When you are located just too far away from Alexa's earshot (or "micshot", please excuse my grammar) or if there is just too much noise inside the house and you do not want to have to shout at Alexa from across the room, then using the microphone incorporated into the remote control device will be your best option.

A good Echo feature that would be so much fun and amusing to use with the remote control device is the "Simon says." This action commands Echo to have Alexa repeat whatever and everything you say. When done using the remote control device as a practical joke launched at an unaware audience such as kids or individuals paranoid with techie gadgets, it could speak tons of laughter. A note of caution though, like any form of practical joke, know your limits and use it only with friendly badgers and learn to stop when you think you have gone too far.

Flash Briefing: With the use of the Amazon Echo you can listen to the most recent news released from a myriad of different sources with your customizations in control and also acquire the latest weather information. These options are all included in its Flash briefing feature and can be accessed by simply saying the prompt words "Alexa, what's my Flash Briefing". Alternatively you can use the phrase "Alexa, what's going on today?"

In order to sift through items and articles in your Flash Briefing, you can use the following phrases for Alexa:

"Alexa, next"

"Alexa, previous"

"Alexa, cancel"

Amazon continues to diversify and enrich this option and recently added news sources such as the highly awarded non-profit multimedia news provider the National Public Radio (NPR), as well as The Economist which is a high caliber source of opinion related to any useful current information gathered either locally, nationally or internationally.

To be able to please a greater proportion of the public, Amazon has even linked their Echo with the "The Thirty Mile Zone" or the TMZ which is one of the most popular sources for the latest news on entertainment and show business.

To customize your Flash Briefing, you will have to log on to your Amazon Alexa account and select or deselect items you want Alexa to consider when you ask her for your Flash Briefing.

Using Echo's Bluetooth Capability: Amazon Echo is first and foremost a useful Bluetooth speaker which can connect to your smart phones or tablets in order to play audio files. To do this, you first need to pair your device with the Echo before starting with your audio streaming.

Pairing the Amazon Echo to your device can be done using the following phrases:

"Alexa, connect my phone" or "Alexa, connect my tablet"

"Alexa, pair Bluetooth"

"Alexa, disconnect my phone" or "Alexa, disconnect my tablet"

Once your device is paired, you can now use the Amazon Echo to control the audio of your device for you. Fans of the famous music streaming app Spotify have been using this feature to play their favorite radio music stations on Echo. Once Spotify in your tablet or phone is already playing in the Echo speakers, talk to Alexa to do the following options for you:

"Alexa, play."

"Alexa, previous."

"Alexa, next."

"Alexa, pause."

"Alexa, resume."

"Alexa, stop."

"Alexa, restart."

As of now, only these options can be used for the Amazon Echo when it is playing via Bluetooth connectivity. If for instance you ask for Alexa to play a certain song, an artist, a playlist or a particular album then Amazon Echo will pause playing from your tablet or mobile device, disconnect the Bluetooth connection and play the requested file using the Amazon Music library. To return to playing via Bluetooth, just start over and ask Alexa to connect Echo with your device over Bluetooth again.

Clock and Timer: Many Amazon Echo users have been finding the clock and timer capability of the device extremely useful. Setting up multiple timers and/or alarms with a simple voice command has never been made more convenient. It is exactly like being back in your university dorm room during final exam week and asking your roommate to wake you up a few minutes after you rest your mind with a power nap. The difference being the Echo will never forget to wake you up or let you down by falling asleep as well. The Amazon Echo is a prompt and very reliable alarm clock which can also double back as a silent timer in the background.

Ask Alexa to do the following commands for you:

"Alexa, what time is it?"

"Alexa, what is the date today?"

"Alexa, set the alarm for 6:30 AM"

"Alexa, wake me up at six thirty in the morning"

"Alexa, when is my alarm set for?"

"Alexa, cancel the alarm for six thirty in the morning"

"Alexa, set the timer for 5 minutes"

"Alexa, cancel the timer for 5 minutes"

"Alexa, how much time is left on my timer?"

"Alexa, snooze"

"Alexa, stop"

You can interrupt Alexa with these commands anytime: There is a set of commands that you can throw at Alexa anytime even while she is still in the middle of a certain task. These commands are the following:

"Alexa, stop"

"Alexa, repeat"

"Alexa, louder"

"Alexa, turn it down"

"Alexa, mute"

"Alexa, unmute"

"Alexa, help"

Voicecast: There is an added feature of the Amazon Echo that is exclusively compatible with the Amazon Fire tablet.

This feature can be considered as an almost analogous attribute to that of Apple's with their effort to make their device as exclusive as possible. This is probably the closest thing Amazon can get to an attempt to set apart their products for exclusive use with their own devices alone.

Voicecast allows any Amazon Echo user to send out additional information about its recent searches to your Fire tablet. Searches such as recent news, the weather updates, Wikipedia information and facts, traffic details and anything else you have additional information to can be sent into your tablet for easy access, provided your tablet is Fire of course.

Here are the phrases you can use to Voicecast and have the Echo beam your desired information to your Fire tablet:

"Alexa, send that to my Fire tablet"

Or you can say it without having to specify it:

"Alexa, send that to my tablet"

And you can even ask Alexa to send the information to another household members Fire tablet (Again, it goes without saying that the tablet should have already been recognized and identified by Alexa and is also linked to the same wireless fidelity):

> "Alexa, send this to Kelly's Fire"

CHAPTER 10 - GAMES, INFO AND FUN THINGS TO ASK ALEXA

The Amazon Echo can be highly productive in your day to day life if you make use of its potential. For example, if you're in the kitchen, making some soup for dinner and you need five cups of chicken broth. Unfortunately all you have is a 40-ounce package chicken broth on hand; you could ponder whether that's just the right amount, too much, or too little.

Why not simply turn to Alexa and ask "Alexa, how many ounces are in five cups?" The Amazon Echo will reply "Five cups is forty fluid ounces," This makes your life easier and you don't have to struggle with making the conversion yourself or wash your hands and go over to your laptop, tablet or computer to Google the correct amounts.

If you need to purchase anything, some milk or cheese for instance, that's running low in the household, all you have to do is say "Alexa, add milk to my shopping list." Alexa will respond, "I've added milk to your shopping list." How awesome is that?

Asking questions will give you a lot of insight and knowledge. This is perfect for the little ones who are always curious and wondering how or why things are the way they are. For instance, you could ask "Alexa, what were you named after?" and she will respond, "I was named after the Library of Alexandria which was a storage of the knowledge of the Ancient world!"

On top of that Alexa can help your child with their homework as long as the questions asked are within the scope of her comprehension.

Here are a variety of other fun stuff and game questions that you can ask Alexa:

'Alexa, what amount of wood would a wood-chuck, if a

wood-chuck could chuck some wood?'

'Alexa, what does the fox say?'

'Alexa, what is your favorite color?'

'Alexa, when were you born?'

'Alexa, will you marry me?'

'Alexa, who was the 10th president of the United States of America?'

'Alexa, what is your favorite food?'

'Alexa, why do we exist?'

'Alexa, what is the meaning of life and death?'

'Alexa, who is your daddy?"

'Alexa, what is the airspeed velocity of an unladen swallow?"

'Alexa, what is your quest?"

'Alexa, who's that Pokemon?'

You can also instruct the Amazon Echo to tell you a few jokes and it will! Just say,

"Alexa, tell me a joke."

Just don't expect Bill Crosby type jokes and you won't be disappointed!

For every simple question that can be easily solved with a verbal answer such as the ones listed above, Alexa automatically replies with her spoken answer. Whenever she can't seem to find the answer to your question, or if she can't understand the question you threw at her, Alexa opens a card in the Echo app and upon your touch signal can be converted into a Bing search.

CHAPTER 11 - PLAYING MUSIC AND PODCASTS

The Amazon Echo comes pre-registered to the account of the individual who ordered it. Therefore, the moment the Echo gains a connection to Wi-Fi, it has instant access to Amazon Prime music services and any music that is stored in your account. This is also inclusive of any digital copies of any particular CDs that the user may have acquired from Amazon in the past.

The Echo can also draw on iHeart Radio, Pandora, TuneIn and recently iTunes and Spotify for musical content via the IFTTT. However, you will need to input your account information in the Amazon Echo app so that these services can be available for you.

To play music as you already know, you will just have to ask Alexa to rock on. For instance, if you want to listen to a playlist that is based on a specific artist; just instruct Alexa to play music by the specific artist. Alexa will then confirm with you what she is about to play. With the Echo, you can also be very specific about the song that you want to listen to, and in addition, you can ask for broad playlists based on different genres of music. If Alexa is ever unclear about your selection, she will ask you for clarification.

Here are a few music and podcast commands that you can easily give Alexa:

- To play a custom-mix that is based on either an artist or genre, available on Pandora and iHeart Radio just say:

"Alexa, play my {artist name or genre} station on {iHeart Radio or Pandora}"

Alternatively, you can open the navigation panel on the left hand side of the Echo app and select either Pandora or iHeart Radio then search for the artist or genre and select to play the station based on the artist or genre you have chosen.

- To play a radio station, you can say:

"Alexa, play {station frequency}," or

"Alexa, play the station {station name}," or

"Alexa, play the station {station call sign}."

You can also use the Echo app for podcasts or programs by simply opening the navigation panel and select TuneIn or iHeart Radio, then search for the station you want or browse the selection highlights.

- To play a program or a podcast, simply say:

"Alexa, play the podcast/program {podcast/program name}."

- It's also possible for you to like or dislike a song that is playing. This feature is only available for custom stations on Pandora and iHeart Radio. All you need to say is:

"Alexa, thumbs up / down." (Off topic: Gladiator much?) or,

"Alexa, I like this song / I don't like this song."

You can also perform this task using the Echo app. From the Now Playing tab, display the current queue, select Queue and choose the song that you want to like or dislike. From there, you can then select the icon of thumbs up or thumbs down.

- Skipping to the next song (only in Pandora and

iHeart Radio)

You can simply instruct Alexa to skip the song by saying "Alexa, skip." Alternatively, you can manually press the skip icon on the Echo app.

> **TIP:** Free Pandora accounts are restricted to only six skips every hour for every station and iHeart Radio accounts are restricted to only 6 skips every hour for every station, for up to fifteen skips daily across all Custom Stations.

Take a frequently played song out of the music rotation (only available in Pandora) by simply instructing Alexa:

"Alexa, I am tired of this song."

You can also go to the Now Playing tab in the Echo app, choose the Queue option so that the current queue is displayed and select the song that you want to take out of the rotation and select "I am tired of this track".

To create a new station, instruct Alexa by saying;

"Alexa, make a station for {artist name}," or

"Alexa, create a Pandora/ iHeart Radio station based on {artist name}."

With the Echo app, you can simply select Pandora or iHeartRadio from the navigation panel on the left and then type the artist that you want into the search bar.

If the music selection you've asked Alexa for is not possible, she will offer alternative suggestions which are similar. For instance, if you instruct Alexa to play something that is not available such as,

"Alexa, play the Beatles on Prime Music,"

and in the highly unlikely event that Amazon Prime Music services doesn't store Beatles music, the immediate response of Alexa will be "There is no Beatles music on Prime Music, shall I play a Beatles station on iHeart Radio instead?" If you say yes, Alexa will start playing the alternative option immediately.

When the music is playing, it's still possible to ask Alexa to adjust the volume, skip, repeat, pause, play and stop any track you are listening to. Any time you call out to Alexa, the speaker automatically reduces the volume of the music so that she can listen to you more clearly.

Audio playback sounds are remarkable on the Amazon Echo. The volume gets up there for a small system which makes Alexa a great addition to house parties, not only that but very little distortion occurs at the higher ranges of volume. It also handles bass quite well, although it's not quite up to scratch with a subwoofer.

Streaming of music via Bluetooth from the Kindle Fire HDX or any supported Android tablet also works very well. It can easily act in the capacity of a dedicated Bluetooth speaker but obviously is even better as it has other functionalities whilst coming in at a cheap price point.

The Bluetooth pairing process is done by voice, simply instruct Alexa to pair up to a device by saying, "Alexa pair my phone." She will talk you through the easy steps and your device will connect to Alexa. Disconnecting the device is also as simple as instructing the Amazon Echo to disconnect your device, i.e. "Alexa, disconnect my phone".

The accuracy of speech recognition on the Echo is impressive, it can clearly listen to voice commands from over 30 feet away even whilst music is playing since the quality and array of the microphone is top of the range.

CHAPTER 12 – SO ALEXA'S BROUGHT HER POPULAR FRIEND IFTTT ALONG WITH HER

This new integration of Amazon Echo with IFTTT has just added a whole lot of actions for the smart speaker. IFTTT is the abbreviation for "If This Then That". To explain it in the easiest way possible, what IFTTT does is provide a user-friendly platform for a number of distinct devices or apps to work together. IFTTT makes a complicated technical procedure seem simple enough for ordinary folk to be able to use it without much fuss.

IFTTT is an incorporated feature that allows Amazon Echo users to devise conditions or rules (called "recipes") that will direct how other devices, websites, and apps function with each other.

These recipes act as the activator that signals or sets off some kind of user-directed action. An example would be IF you ask the Amazon Echo to make a purchase for you THEN you receive the purchase details in the form of a private message sent to your Gmail account. You get to create these connections by means of connecting channels from the official IFTTT website. With over a hundred of these channels available you can make thousands of connections enabling you to do inexhaustible functions and the only limit would be your creativity.

In order to tap into this powerful function of the IFTTT, Amazon has recently added the Amazon Alexa channel into this long channel list. The Amazon Alexa channel allows you to create recipes and do connections with other channels in the IFTTT.

To begin using third party applications with your Amazon Echo using the IFTTT you first need to activate the Amazon Alexa Channel on the official IFTTT website. After successful activation, you can then get started with creating your very own recipes. As of now, Amazon Echo is designed to only be the trigger in the recipe created and is not yet built to be the result of an action. By means of example, it is not yet possible for you to set up Echo to notify you whenever you receive an email in your Gmail account.

If you find yourself still grasping for more direction in setting up the IFTTT functionality, you can learn from the following sample recipes that may be very handy for your Amazon Echo:

- If you ask Amazon Echo to review your calendar, then you receive an SMS with a complete list of everything you have scheduled for the day.
- If you accomplish a task on your To-do list, then Echo will write a post for you on your spouse's Facebook wall.
- If you finish a good book using the Echo, then all members in your Book Club will receive an email in their Gmail.
- If you give a song currently playing through your Echo a thumbs up, then this preference will be tweeted to your followers on Twitter.

You can create tons of recipes, literally anything you can think of. All you have to do is find an available channel on the IFTTT website and check the things it can do.

Creating new recipes is fairly simple and made even easier with the user friendly interface of the IFTTT website. All you have to do to get started is to log in to your IFTTT account on the Amazon Alexa Channel. The "Create" option can be seen on the webpage to start with creating a recipe. Then select the "Amazon Alexa Channel" on the "this" portion of the ifthisthenthat of the website. You can now "Create Trigger" by selecting from the list of Action Channels and clicking the "that" part of the ifthisthenthat. "Activate Channel" and create the action that you want Amazon Echo to trigger. You can then add "ingredients" or the added details you want to input into your recipe. The ingredients are all dependent on the app or service you want to use. Finalize your recipe by clicking on "Create Action".

Now that you have gotten the basics of recipe creation, it's time to start inventing your very own fun IFTTT action and get busy cooking! Don't forget to spread your blessings and share some of your favorite useful recipes to the growing community of Echo users.

CHAPTER 13 – LET ALEXA HAVE HER WAY IN THE HOUSE

Among all the state of the art features the Amazon Echo has got up its sleeves, or should I say inside its cylindrical metal cover, this latest one is probably the most technologically advanced and one that gives us a few power shoves into our leap towards the computer driven future.

Thanks to Amazon's partnership with huge companies providing smart home devices such as Belkin's WeMo, Philips Hue, SmartThings and WINK, you can now power up your home appliances with a verbal command.

To activate this set up, all the smart devices such as light bulbs, power outlets and hubs must first be connected to your home's wireless fidelity network and then each one named. You can give unique practical names such as

"Bedroom lamp shade", "Garage ceiling light", and "Coffeemaker." Then, make sure that all these smart devices are paired with the Amazon Echo. This will enable you to command Alexa to power on or off each individual device. You can ask her to "turn on the coffeemaker" or "turn off the garage ceiling light".

Furthermore, it would be convenient to group together devices located in the same room or area and group devices of the same kind. You can designate an area in the house as a particular zone and cluster together all devices in that zone. For example you can first group all lights in your household under the group "Lights" then assign all living room light bulbs into the "Living Room" zone. This would allow you to issue a single command for a number of devices grouped together under a single name.

For example, talk to Alexa and ask her to "turn off all lights" and you will suddenly find yourself devoid of any light source wherever you are in the house. But instruct Alexa to "turn off all lights in the living room" and only that section of the house will be exposed to the dark.

Other devices with this smart function can also be dimmed through a voice command given to Alexa. You can say "Alexa dim the Living Room lights" and Echo will dim the lights to a relative degree. Or you can specify this command with an "Alexa dim the Living Room lights to 30 per cent" and you will get your request accurately.

Here is a list of some useful phrases you can utilize when getting the Amazon Echo to connect to your home devices:

"Alexa, discover my devices"

"Alexa, turn on the living room television"

"Alexa, turn off the outdoor Christmas lights"

CHAPTER 14 – WOAH. HOW FLEXIBLE IS ALEXA?

Any question that has a simple, spoken answer, like the time, the weather forecast, or the date of birth of your favorite singer, Alexa is able to provide. If she can't find the answer, or doesn't understand the question, she will create a card in the Echo app and in all other Kindle products as well as the Android OS and iOS. Your query goes into that card, and then with a single tap you can load up a Bing search (unfortunately there is currently no other search engine options). The Echo app contains a chronological history of all your questions, to-do and shopping lists you have ever asked as well as a variety of useful tips for how to communicate with Alexa. For any of you excel spreadsheet geeks this is an awesome feature for you to track your spending habits as you have a bread crumb trail of where money is flowing out of your pockets!

Alexa also has the ability to handle multiple speakers well. You can invite friends over and they will all be able to give Alexa commands and ask questions. Alexa will hear each one without failing, and will respond to each command or question.

Amazon has utilized an exceptionally broad language foundation to begin with, and the Echo is able to expand upon this foundation gradually through use as it learns. Amazon also has the ability to spread out its language base together with the features at any given time, because it is always connected to the World Wide Web.

This language recognition is also assisted by the creation of pseudo profiles for each individual, since Echo has the ability to distinguish the person adding something to a to-do list based off the voice profile it has recognized.

The fact that it can accurately tell you the weather of your location means that it already knows where you reside since you don't have to keep saying where you are unless you want to know the weather forecast of a different location. This is merely the tip of the iceberg, the Echo technology which is supported by the immense cloud and battalion of data scientists from Amazon also has the ability to determine the following:

- Unique occupants of a specific home:

Echo can distinguish between the number of unique voices in your household, if it listens and hears the same voices a lot, it can determine how many individuals live in your house.

- Home visitors:

Since Echo can know who lives in the house, it is also be able to figure out how many home visitors you have.

- Gender and age:

Our individual voices carry distinct patterns and this also enables the Echo determine our gender as well as our probable age.

- Emotion detection:

Same as gender, our voices carry specific patterns whenever we are happy, sad, or angry. Therefore, the Echo is able to detect this which is an odd functionality to have but imagine in the future if it would be able to report to you the percentage of time in the past week that you spent in a happy, peaceful or sad mood. This would be great for self-introspection, therapy and many other uses.

- Who's at home:

Since the Amazon Echo has the ability to create pseudo profiles and is able to detect the sounds of a door opening or closing, gradually, it will be able to determine who is physically at home and who isn't. This could be somewhat difficult if no one is talking, but with time, Echo will have the ability to match a pattern against what a unique individual does once they come in through the door.

For instance, do they clod around, barely make a single sound or do they drag their feet? Do they first head to the fridge or walk upstairs? Since we are creatures of habit as human beings, these patterns are not that difficult for Alexa to register. The sound of our gait or the stride of our length could also be determined.

- What we listen to and watch:

If the Amazon Echo can hear the music and TV in the background, it can determine what is playing and eventually determine your preferences.

CHAPTER 15 – OOPS, I PUSHED HER WRONG BUTTONS (TROUBLESHOOTING)

In the event that Alexa has any issues whilst you are using her, below are a selection of the most common issues and how to solve them;

1. **If Alexa is not understanding you:**

- Ensure there's no background noise when you're speaking to the Echo.
- Speak slowly and clearly.
- Use the Amazon Echo remote to provide commands.
- Complete Voice Training so that your Amazon

Echo can understand you better.

- Check the suggested phrases for different types of requests.
- Continue using it and it will improve over time as it acclimatizes to your speech patterns.

2. If Alexa plays the wrong song:

You should check the music log in the Echo app to see what Alexa heard you say. If it heard you properly, but didn't play the right song, then you most likely don't have the song you requested in your library or it may not be present within Prime Music. You may also want to check what program is currently selected in your Echo app as your song may be in Pandora whilst the Echo app is currently tuned into iHeartRadio.

3. Alexa is not able to answer your questions:

- You should try repeating the question since Amazon Echo might have misheard you.
- You can also rephrase the question that you asked.
- You can try to be more specific or more general with the question that you have attempted to ask.
- If the Amazon Echo does not realize that you have asked a question, you can attempt by starting the question with the phrase "question".
- For example, you would say "Alexa, question, {phrase your question here}."

TIP: The Amazon Echo does not know ALL answers (yet) to all the available questions you can think of. Try visiting the Amazon site to look for examples of questions that the Echo can answer, they are constantly updated when new updates are released for the Echo.

4. Amazon Echo Remote failing to connect.

- Confirm that the remote has 2 x AAA batteries inserted.
- Go to the Settings panel and then pair remote in the Echo app, and then long-press the Play button (or hold the button for 5 seconds) while the Echo is still searching.
- If a purple light that is spinning is seen on your device, this means that more than a single remote was detected. Press the Play button on the remote that you want to use to connect to the Echo.

TIP: Only a single Amazon Echo Remote can be paired with the Echo at a given time.

5. If you forgot 'Your Confirmation Code':

- First ensure you clearly speak the confirmation code to the Echo to make sure you haven't actually 'forgotten' what the code is!
- In the Echo app, go to the Settings and in the

navigation panel, go to the left side and select Voice Purchasing.

- Enter a fresh confirmation code and then save the changes you have made.

TIP: Never use the same code that you use for your Amazon Echo for any other services that you have.

6. If the Amazon Echo Can't Connect to Wi-Fi

- If you're not sure whether your Amazon Echo has been connected to a Wi-Fi network, look at the power LED at the base of the device. The power LED located above the power chord displays the Wi-Fi state of your device:

a) A solid white light at the base of your Amazon Echo indicates that it is connected to a Wi-Fi network.

b) A solid orange light shows that the Amazon Echo has not been connected to a Wi-Fi network.

c) A blinking orange light indicates that your Amazon Echo has been connected to a Wi-Fi network, but has not yet connected to the cloud, if so give it a few minutes to connect into the cloud.

For diagnostics, you should try this first:

- Reconnect to the Wi-Fi network.
- Ensure that you have input the Wi-Fi password of the network in correctly. (If a network password is required, you will see the icon of a Lock). Note that you don't input your Amazon account password here, it requires the password for your Wi-Fi Network to connect.
- You should also ensure that the connection of your internet isn't down. To solve this issue, you can attempt to restart your modem or your router and if this doesn't work, you may want to contact your internet service provider for a status update.
- You can also move the Amazon Echo closer to

your modem or router if they aren't within the same room or in case there's interruption occurring between the router and Echo.

If you are still experiencing troubles after performing the above then you should:

- Disconnect the Amazon Echo's power cord for 3 seconds, and then plug it in again.
- Ensure that your Echo has been registered to your own Amazon account. Go to your Amazon Account online and go to the 'Manage Your Content and Devices' setting.

Then select 'Your Devices'. Look for the Amazon Echo's name here. From here, you can, deregister your Amazon Echo simply by selecting the 'Deregister' option under your Amazon Echo's name. After that, set up your Amazon Echo again. Failing this, contact Amazon and they will gladly assist you!

CHAPTER 16 - CONCLUSION

This book is a special composition for those who have already purchased the Amazon Echo (or are tossing up whether or not to purchase one!). You will be able to easily unlock the full potential of your exceptional device without any troubles. This guide can be an easy reference for you to have an easy time with:

- Controlling your music
- Asking questions, about the news, weather, traffic and general knowledge information
- Managing your shopping and to-do lists
- Managing your alarms and timers
- Managing your settings across your Amazon

account and the Echo app

- Viewing the history of the commands and questions you have ever asked
- Navigating the Echo App

Thank you again for purchasing this book and taking your time to read this book, feel free to refer back to it and also don't forget your free bonuses which includes a list of example questions you can ask for easy reference on the next page!

I hope the guide has helped you and provided value in your pursuit of completely understanding how the Amazon Echo works. I also hope that you will find the tips and tricks provided helpful as you incorporate this device into your day to day life.

The next step is to take advantage of whatever you have learnt and use it in the easy operation of your Amazon Echo! **Thank you and good luck!**

CHAPTER 17 – FREE BONUS :)

For your free bonus gift: ***Amazon Echo Cheat Sheet: 64 Amazon Echo Commands & Questions*** type the link below into your web browser:

http://bit.ly/EchoBonus

Enjoy!!!

Please find below a bonus sneak peek preview of *OneNote: Getting Things Done Like David Allen with OneNote* by Jack Echo which is available now on Amazon!

SNEAK PEEK PREVIEW: Getting Things Done Productivity System (2015)

If you've never heard of Getting Things Done (GTD) before then you're in for a treat. GTD is a work-life management system devised by David Allen that was first published in 2001 under the same name. In March 2015, David Allen released a revised and updated version of his International Bestseller taking into account the rapid onset of technological advancements, cognitive scientific research and their implications on the GTD system and our productivity. I'll be covering some of these cognitive research studies later on.

The GTD system was developed to bring order to chaos so that you can achieve stress-free productivity. You can think of the GTD system much like highway codes and road names, the only twist here is to apply the same concept to organizational skills. Without highway codes or road names, cars would drive in all sorts of directions and nobody would ever get anywhere or if you did manage to finally get somewhere it wouldn't have been in the most efficient manner possible - the same thing is most likely occurring in your life if you don't have a productivity system in place!

Most people find they're incredibly busy, and it's no wonder with so many things vying for our attention (have you noticed the substantial amount of billboards, TV ads and online pop up ads with companies basically jumping in front of your face shouting "pick me, pick me, pick me!").

It's no surprise that being able to stay organized in this world is incredibly difficult – just think about the stacks or piles of paper you have scattered around your work space or office, as well as the many things you have bouncing around in your head at this single moment in time… Things that you have to-do, people you have to get back to and urgent reminders you have to juggle inside of your head so you don't forget to complete them.

One of the main goals and priorities of the GTD system is to get EVERYTHING you need to do out of your head so that you can operate with a "mind like water" thus allowing you to easily enter into the "zone" or flow state where things are done seamlessly and almost effortlessly. This concept first derived from athletes that would enter into a state termed "flow" during their performances. Athletes would often find they were no longer consciously performing yet everything would flow smoothly and effortlessly. This concept is detailed thoroughly in *Flow* by Mihaly Csikszentmihalyi and more recently a practical application of the concept has been detailed in Stephen Kotler's, *The Rise of Superman: Decoding the Science of Ultimate Human Performance.* The underlying principle here is to not be a human doing that is constantly thinking about the things you need to do, but rather to be a human BEING that does the things you ought to be doing in the present moment without niggling thoughts running through your mind.

The idea of having a "mind like water" derives from karate, where you're required to clear your mind and relax in order to achieve the appropriate levels of strength and power for optimal efficiency (**Fun fact:** David Allen is a Karate black belt). If you ever find yourself operating from a tense and anxious state, you'll notice that in retrospect operating from this state narrows your perspective and impairs your ability to accomplish tasks efficiently. This is the same for karate and other sports, when your muscles are too tense you operate with less flexibility, less range of motion, and your ability to perform at your greatest potential decreases. People who don't have a “mind like water” often respond inappropriately to situations because they are controlled by situations that cause them to underreact or overreact given the context for a situation. As you can imagine, responding inappropriately to situations leads to suboptimal results.

Our brains were not made to function as storage spaces, they were made to think creatively and find solutions to issues. It’s been found that having to store things diminishes our clarity and focus and hence our productivity. In the 2008 research paper *Getting Things Done: The Science Behind Stress-Free Productivity* written by two researchers from Belgium who analyzed the GTD methodology, the researchers came to the profound conclusion that your mind is designed to have ideas based upon pattern recognition, but it isn’t designed to remember much of anything. This is due to the way the mind developed in prehistoric times and as a result our minds are brilliant at recognition, but terrible at recall.

This finding is further supported in Daniel Levitin's *The Organized Mind* which emphasizes that when you use your memory as your organizing system, your mind will effectively become overwhelmed and incompetent as it is working at a higher intensity level due to performing work it's not suited for. Another interesting cognitive science conclusion brought to light by Dr Roy Baumeister is that the completion of uncompleted tasks does not relieve the burden on the psyche of having to remember these uncompleted tasks. What is needed is a trusted plan that ensures forward engagement will occur which is the core of the GTD system.

Once you have the GTD system in place you will have a fool proof system for keeping track of the things you need to do, should do or are *thinking about* doing and this provides you with the mental clarity and space for you to focus on the things that matter and also enhance your likelihood of entering "flow" or operating with a "mind like water" as you undertake your work.

"The art of resting the mind and the power of dismissing from it all care and worry is probably one of the secrets of our great men"

– Captain J. A. Hatfield

The three key objectives of the GTD system are to:

1. **Capture all the things that might need to get done or have usefulness for you – now, later, someday, big, little, or in between – in a logical and trusted system outside your head and off your mind**
2. **Directing yourself to make front-end decisions about all of the "inputs" you let into your life so that you will always have a workable inventory of "next actions" that you can implement or renegotiate in the moment**
3. **Curating and coordinating all of the content, utilizing the recognition of the multiple levels of commitments with yourself and others that you have at play, at any single point in time.**

To begin with, we will discuss the context of the lists

that are used in the GTD system that we will learn how to set up in OneNote in Chapter 7. The contexts of these lists are provided first so you can gain an understanding of them before we start implementing them, from this understanding you gain an idea of why and what these lists are used for:

The "In" (or Capture) List

This list will hold and capture all your ideas or tasks as they come to you (literally or figuratively), for example, if your boss asks you get his suit dry cleaned you'll put this into your "in" list or if you remember that you've scheduled a coffee catch up with Mike but forgot to note it down in your calendar – you'll put these ideas or tasks into your "in" list. These items/ideas/tasks are all considered to be "open loops" – anything that does not belong where it is, the way it is will pull on your attention if it's not appropriately managed and as such are open loops until they are complete or finished.

If this is your first time implementing an organizational system you'll want to set aside time the near future (at least

2 hours - some people have taken up to 6 hours and longer to do this) and write down ALL, yes, I do mean ALL of the different things that currently aren't the way you want them to be. This includes things you will need to do, to things you've been meaning to do.

This may seem like a daunting task at first but trust me, it's worth it and is a lot easier to do then you would expect (and quite fun as well once you get into the groove of it).

After the initial set up and processing of your "in" list (which we get into later), this list serves as the list that captures everything that comes to you. From here, the ideas or tasks on your "in" list will be processed once a day, or every other day. This process is the backbone of the GTD system and will enable you to enhance your efficiency and streamline your actions.

How to Process Your "In" List in 3 Steps

After you've written down all the possible tasks that you could think of, you'll go through each item on your "in" list one at a time. It's important that you go through the list in the order in which you wrote them down so you don't get lost or confused and more importantly, so you don't place higher importance on an item which may eventually sidetrack you from doing the task at hand - which is to process your "in" list. Once you have the item from your "in" list in front of you, you need to ask yourself a series of questions.

1. **"Is it actionable?"**

   This question is asked so that you can determine if you're able to perform a clear, physical and specific action that will achieve the outcome desired. If the answer is no, you either get rid of it (delete it), move it to your reference list, or put it into a someday/maybe list (both lists will be discussed later).

2. **If the answer is yes, then you need to ask "What is the next action?"**

   This action needs to be something you can actually perform; it needs to be a physical and visible action. For example: make a call, type up the report or sign off on the award agreement. Don't specify an action that is vague such as "plan for the competition" make it clear and specific such as "email Dave for the competition entry price." It's always better to be clear and specific when it comes to next actions.

By spending time coming up with a physical AND visible action you will make sure that your 'Next Actions' list is filled with ACTIONABLE items that you can pick up and do at any time. This increases the likelihood that you'll accomplish the actions significantly as you know exactly what you need to do, and all you are required to do is just do it! Without a next action, there remains a potentially infinite gap between the current reality and what you need to do to accomplish the intended outcome. The best way to close this gap is to write down the very next physical action required that will move the current situation forward. If you had nothing else to do in your life but get closure on this, what visible action would you take right now? Once you have defined the specific next action move on to…

3. **Asking yourself, "Will this action take less than 2 minutes to complete?"**

If the answer is yes – drop everything and do it straight away!

If the answer is no, you either delegate it to someone more appropriate to undertake the action. You can do this by writing down who you've delegated the task to and making a note of this in your waiting for list, otherwise you will defer the next action by putting it into the 'Next Actions' list.

The 2 minute rule depends on your own circumstances and time available, if you're short on time to process your "in" list, you can lower it to 30 seconds. If you have more time then you can increase it to 5 or 10 minutes.

Remember triple D when it comes to processing your "in" list and you won't go wrong: Do it, Delegate it or Defer it.

You can only feel good about what you're not doing when you know everything you're not doing.

Three Reasons Things Are on Your Mind

Remember, most often the reason that something is on your mind is because you want something to be different than what it currently is and you haven't:

1. Clarified exactly what the outcome is;
2. Decided what the very next physical action step is to change it; or
3. Put reminders of the outcome and the action required in a system you trust.

Any "would, could, or should" commitment held only in the psyche creates irrational and unresolvable pressure, 24-7.

This is why the "Next Actions" list is so powerful at moving us forward...

"Next Actions" List

This is a list of your... well... next actions, believe it or not! This is the list you will refer to once you've finished a task you were previously working on or require a new task to start working on. From here, you'll determine the next action to complete off this list based on what's most appropriate for the given context, time, energy and focus you have available. Rinse and repeat this process and you become a productivity machine!

A quick tip for determining when the next action is done comes down to two basic components that are required:

1. Defining what done means (the outcome); and
2. What doing looks like (the specific, physical action).

You will most likely end up with 25-150+ next actions depending on how many items you initially captured in your in list. The more next actions you have, the better it is to build sub-lists within your next actions list which will be broken down by contexts (refer to below) that separate your next actions and divides them into more manageable groups.

There is usually an inverse relationship between how much something is on your mind and how much it's getting done.

"Waiting For" List

This is a list of things that you're waiting for someone else to complete. This list can comprise a number of things, mainly it will be for work you've delegated to someone else, an email you're waiting on a reply to or work that requires input from someone else before it can be completed.

The most important part of this list is that you review it weekly or as often as you need to so that these actions you've delegated aren't running around rampant in your mind. A great tip for this list is to ensure you note down the date at which the action was delegated to the appropriate person AND write down when you expect the action to be completed by. This makes it easier for you when you need to chase people up in the near future.

END OF SNEAK PREVIEW

INDEX

N

P

Q

R

S

T

U

V

W

Z

Made in the USA
Middletown, DE
05 December 2015